D0708365

# PERTHSHIRE

*A pictorial souvenir*

NESS PUBLISHING

2    In mountainous northern Perthshire, with the pleasingly symmetrical shape of Beinn a' Ghlo ('hill of mist') taking centre stage. Glen Tilt lies between the foreground and the mountain.

# PERTHSHIRE

### Welcome to Perthshire!

Perthshire is a county of contrasts and records: here you will find Britain's tallest tree, the world's tallest hedge (opposite), the smallest distillery and the oldest living thing in Europe, if not on the planet! From the city of Perth with its population of approximately 43,000 to tiny highland villages like Kinloch Rannoch, it embraces communities of all sizes. A largely rural county, its landscape includes rich farmland growing everything from grain to soft fruit and, at the other end of the spectrum, some of Scotland's wildest country. Ben Lawers, Scotland's tenth highest peak, towers over the expanse of Loch Tay, while the northern parts of the county are home to some of the country's most inaccessible Munros (mountains over 3,000ft/914m). Whatever your taste in scenery, it will be found somewhere in this characterful county.

Perthshire has witnessed more than its share of Scotland's history-in-the-making, with kings enthroned on Moot Hill, former location of the Stone of Scone, just north of Perth. Going back to earlier times, the Picts told their stories through carvings in standing stones, some of which have survived to provide the county with perhaps its most fascinating relics. We shall see one of the most important of these on p.31. Many of Scotland's most famous – and notorious – personalities have made their name or left their mark here: the bard Ossian; Macbeth; William Wallace; Robert the Bruce; Mary, Queen of Scots; Rob Roy MacGregor; Bonnie Prince

Left: Meikleour beech hedge, 30 metres/100 ft high and 530 metres/third-of-a-mile long stretches **5** along the A93 south of Blairgowrie. Right: 1885 drinking fountain, The Square, Aberfeldy.

Charlie; Sir Walter Scott. Some say that Pontius Pilate was born in the village of Fortingall, Glen Lyon (see p.52).

This book aims to convey something of that variety by means of a photographic tour around the county. Starting in the city of Perth itself, we then investigate its environs before setting off to explore further afield. We shall cross the county a number of times, starting by working from east to west across its southern districts, then heading north for a while before crossing back from west to east through the central area. From the eastern side there will be another step north, before a final east-to-west transit through the mountains and along the lochs to the north-west corner of Perthshire.

It should be said that, like all other counties, Perthshire's boundaries have changed somewhat over the years. In recent times it has lost its south-western part to Stirling, but we shall dip into this area in acknowledgement of its recent past. Conversely, Perthshire absorbed the former county of Kinross to the south; however, we shall not venture there as this area falls more naturally into another region of Scotland that will be the subject of a later book in this series. For similar reasons, one or two of its most easterly outposts that, historically, have more connection with the county of Angus will be included in the book for that area.

The city of Perth can trace its roots back to the 10th century, a settlement being established there about 150 years before it became a royal burgh around 1124. It was a natural place for a settlement, at the lowest fording (later, bridging) point of Scotland's longest and most volatile river, the Tay. The aerial picture opposite gives a good idea of the city's layout, looking south. The numbers refer to the page in this book on which that building/feature is illustrated.

Perth from the air. The circular building with a blue roof at bottom right is the new Concert Hall. 7
The numbers mark the location of places illustrated in this book – see last paragraph opposite.

8    From Perth Bridge, looking north along the Tay with North Inch Park on the far side of the river.

10 An interesting contrast in shapes reaching to the sky: a modern sculpture in the Norrie-Miller Park on the east bank of the Tay, and across the river St Matthew's Church.

The same park exhibits a number of such sculptures, **11**
which reward investigation of their thought-provoking shapes.

12 Perth Bridge, built in 1766 by John Smeaton and widened in 1869 by A.D. Stewart. The Tay has demolished a number of earlier bridges on or near this site.

A view from Perth Bridge looking south along Tay Street. **13**
The buildings show off a fine array of finials and other forms of ornamentation.

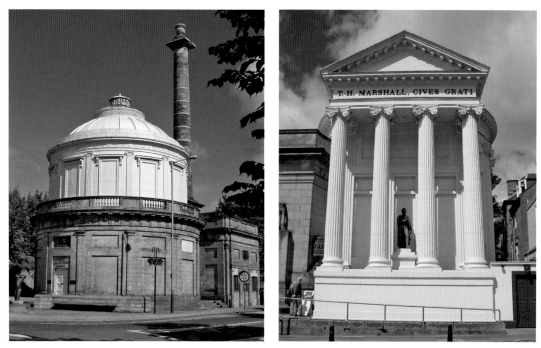

**14** Left: The old water-pumping station built in 1822 is now the Fergusson Gallery, home to the largest collection of work by the Scottish artist, John Duncan Fergusson. Right: Perth Museum & Art Gallery.

Fine and Applied Art displayed at Perth Museum and Art Gallery, one of the oldest museums in 15 the UK with more than half-a-million objects in its Recognised Collection of National Significance.

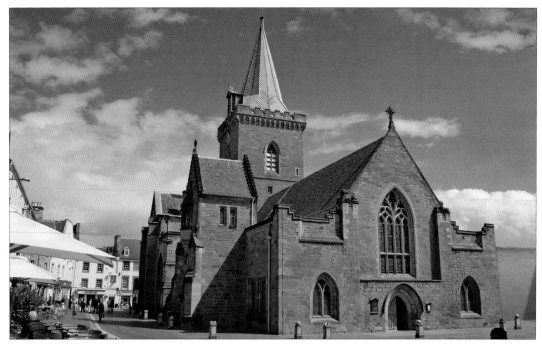

16  St John's Kirk is the oldest standing building in Perth and one of the most important parish churches in Scotland. The original building was completed in 1241 and the leaded spire in place by 1511.

The interior of St John's. The best-known incident to take place here was John Knox's sermon against **17** idolatry preached in 1559. The church underwent a major restoration in 1923. Inset: roof boss.

**18** St John's Street, to the east of the Kirk, demonstrates fine architecture and a variety of sculptures attached to the lamp posts.

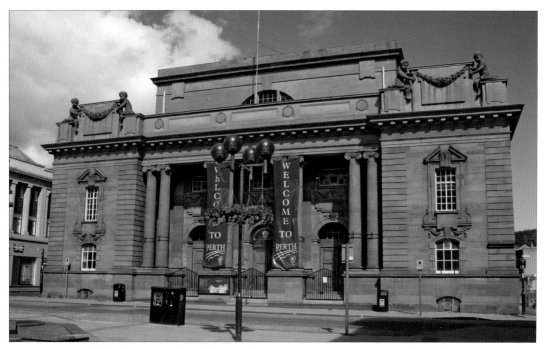

Perth City Hall. This impressive building is undergoing a regeneration project that will turn it into a **19** specialist shopping and restaurant complex. Note the statues at top left and top right of the building.

20 Known as the Fair Maid's House, on North Port, this ancient dwelling is so named because of its fanciful connection to the heroine of *The Fair Maid of Perth* by Sir Walter Scott (1771 - 1832).

Left: the 18th-century Hal o' the Wynd House, West Mill St., also features in the novel *The Fair* **21**
*Maid of Perth*. Right: This memorial in the North Inch pays tribute to the 51st Highland Division.

**22** Branklyn Garden ablaze with autumn colours; it contains over 3,000 plant species in just under 1.75 acres. Now a National Trust for Scotland property, it was created by John and Dorothy Renton.

In the foreground is Perth harbour. Beyond, eastern Perthshire stretches away along the 23 Tay estuary almost to Dundee. On the left is the famous viewpoint of Kinnoull Hill.

**24** A closer look at the dramatic cliffs and steep wooded slopes of Kinnoull Hill with the River Tay and some rich farmland in the foreground.

And from Kinnoull Hill: the folly on the left was built in the 19th century. A patch of sunlight **25** shows up the countryside colours around Kinfauns Castle (a private estate).

**26** Scone Palace, just north of Perth. In 1803 the 3rd Earl of Mansfield employed William Atkinson to rebuild the medieval house into a gothic palace with echoes of the monastic original.

The Drawing Room at Scone. Its Regency opulence is accentuated by treasures from Versailles, **27** most notably the writing desk seen at bottom left of the picture, presented by Marie Antoinette.

**28** Stanley Mills, a few miles north of Scone, began textile manufacturing in 1787 and were in production until 1989. Recently restored, they are open to the public as a Historic Scotland site.

Just east of Perth on the south side of the Tay stands Elcho Castle, a remarkably complete **29** 16th-century fortified mansion. Open to visitors under the auspices of Historic Scotland.

**30** Now moving just west of Perth, Huntingtower Castle comprises two fine and complete tower houses. Also known as The House of Ruthven, it is another excellent Historic Scotland location.

Left: The village of Forteviot was rebuilt in 1925-26 on the site of a Pictish capital, burial place **31** of Kenneth MacAlpin, first King of Scots. Right: the Dupplin Cross in St Serf's Church, Dunning.

**32** Continuing south-west from Perth we reach the town of Auchterarder, which enjoys fine views of the Ochil Hills, seen here in the last light of an autumn evening.

The world-famous Gleneagles golf courses have been providing one of the finest settings **33** for the sport for 90 years. The Gleneagles Hotel opened in 1924.

**34** A real rarity: Tullibardine Chapel is one of the most complete and unaltered medieval churches in Scotland, founded in 1446. It is located two miles north-west of Auchterarder.

Continuing north-west we come to the pleasant village of Muthill and the interesting ruins of **35** another important medieval church. The Romanesque tower is similar to that of Dunning church.

36  Innerpeffray Library near Muthill is the oldest free public lending library in Scotland, founded in 1680. The present building dates to 1762 and contains about 5,000 books.

And now the oldest malt whisky distillery: Glenturret, just outside Crieff, **37** was established in 1775 and is the home of the Famous Grouse.

38 Crieff is the main town of Strathearn, with a population of almost 6,000 and lying on the southern edge of the Scottish Highlands. This is James Square that marks the town centre.

Crieff has been a holiday resort since Victorian times and is the second largest town in Perthshire. 39
The turrets of the famous Crieff Hydro can be seen on the skyline of this picture.

40  Drummond Castle, between Muthill and Crieff, was built around 1490 and its gardens initially laid
out in the early 17th century by John Drummond, 2nd Earl of Perth. After the Second World War,

with a reduced workforce, the decision was taken to simplify the gardens; however, with their ancient **41**
yew hedges and copper beeches, they remain some of the finest formal gardens in Scotland.

**42** North of Crieff, and running roughly west to east, Glen Almond is one of the county's most scenic glens. Even after the heather, it presents a palette of rich colours on the contours of the hills.

A few miles east of the previous view, the River Almond cascades fiercely through the **43** falls at Buchanty Spout, near the village of the same name.

**44** The attractive village of Comrie is west of Crieff on the River Earn and the Highland Boundary Fault. Seismic activity does not seem to affect its Scotland in Bloom success!

Built in 1805 'The White Church' is a Grade A listed building lying at the heart of this **45** historic conservation village. In 1965 it became the village community centre.

46 A few miles further west, St Fillans is exquisitely sited at the eastern end of Loch Earn, seen here stretching into the mountainous distance.

From former Perthshire territory west of Loch Earn, we now look east down steep Glen Ogle to **47** mighty Ben Vorlich, 985m/3232ft. The old railway track-bed can just be seen, bottom right.

**48** Perthshire also used to include the town of Callander, above which Ben Ledi (879m/2885ft) provides a perfect place for viewing Ben Lawers (1214m/3983ft), about 20 miles away to the north.

The delightful village of Killin at the head of Loch Tay also now belongs to Stirling District, but many **49** residents still feel allied to Perthshire. Ben Lawers, in the background, remains in Perthshire.

**50** At the other (eastern) end of Loch Tay is the Scottish Crannog Centre, where an example of this Iron Age type of loch dwelling has been re-constructed to enable visitors a taste of this life.

From the hillside above the Crannog, the village of Kenmore looks appealing in its surrounding **51** gown of autumn colours. A great location from which to explore the county.

**52** Fortingall village in Glen Lyon is where you find this ancient Yew tree: Europe's – and possibly the world's – oldest living thing. Scholars believe its roots go back as much as 5,000 years.

Glen Lyon lies to the north of Loch Tay and is lined by mountains. Here, Creag Mhor (981m/3218ft) **53** stands imposingly above Fortingall. Cairn Mairg (1041m/ 3415ft) lurks beyond in the mist.

**54** Journeying east down Strath Tay brings us to Castle Menzies, seat of Clan Menzies for over 400 years. Prince Charles Edward Stuart's death mask can be seen here.

It's just a short distance on to Aberfeldy, entered via Lt. General Wade's bridge, opened to traffic **55** at the end of October 1733. Almost 400ft in overall length, the centre arch measures 60ft.

56 From above Kenmore, this view looks north-east across Strath Tay – Loch Tay is to the left and Aberfeldy to the right of this scene. The hills in the distance have an early covering of snow.

58 On the edge of Aberfeldy, Dewar's World of Whisky offers an interactive exhibition that educates and entertains. The experience includes a guided distillery tour and whisky tasting.

Continuing south-east along the Tay on route to Dunkeld, this verdant scene **59** captures the agricultural richness of the Strath.

60　The historic town of Dunkeld has much to see including the Ell Shop (left), named after the weaver's measure on the wall outside. Inset: Ell shop detail referring to the National Trust for Scotland.

Dunkeld was proclaimed the first ecclesiastical capital of Scotland by Scotland's first king, Kenneth **61** MacAlpin. The majestic ruin of the cathedral still dominates Dunkeld today. (See also back cover)

**62** The Loch of the Lowes near Dunkeld is a wildlife reserve with a visitor centre run by the Scottish Wildlife Trust. Many bird species including ospreys can be seen, as well as red squirrels.

Left: across the river Tay from Dunkeld is the Hermitage, home of Britain's tallest tree and the **63** Black Linn Falls, pictured here from Ossian's Hall. Right: the River Ericht in Blairgowrie.

**64**  The textile town of Blairgowrie is 11 miles east of Dunkeld. This is the Wellmeadow which, complete with the War Memorial, forms an attractive centrepiece to the town.

The way north from Blairgowrie takes us up famous Glen Shee, at the head of which Perthshire meets **65** Aberdeenshire amid the Cairngorm mountains. Here is a typical scene near Spittal of Glenshee.

66 An idyllic setting for Edradour Distillery, Scotland's smallest. It is situated just off the route from Glen Shee which brings us westwards over the hills to Pitlochry. Visitors welcome.

And in Pitlochry, the historic Blair Athol Distillery also welcomes visitors and treats them to a **67** sample of the produce. That aside, the distilleries have much charm and architectural interest.

68 Pitlochry is spectacularly set amid the Perthshire hills, with Ben Vrackie (840m/2755ft) forming a splendid backdrop and offering a tempting hill walk.

Beautiful Loch Faskally sits beside Pitlochry. The hydro-power dam which created the loch **69** has a salmon ladder alongside it, giving visitors the chance to see these fish in action.

70 The story behind Pitlochry's Festival Theatre can be traced back to the vision arising from John Stewart's visit to the town in 1944. Today's theatre building was opened in 1981.

Killiecrankie Pass, north of Pitlochry, echoed to the sound of battle in July 1689. Redcoat soldier Donald McBane escaped by making a spectacular leap across the river at this point.

72 A scene which captures the upland essence of Perthshire. On the road east from Pitlochry, looking into upper Strath Ardle above the village of Straloch, the hills beckon.

74 Up-river from Killiecrankie, perhaps the ultimate evocation of the fairy-tale fortress: magnificent Blair Castle stands in splendour amidst a scenic symphony that creates a perfect view.

There is so much to enjoy and do at Blair Castle that many visitors return again and again, always discovering something new. This is the magnificent drawing room.

76 The estate village of Blair Atholl: low evening sun highlights the lines of the sturdy but stylish buildings. The village is also home to the Atholl Country Life Museum.

For many, Queen's View (referring to Queen Isabella, wife of Robert the Bruce), Loch Tummel, presents **77** the perfect blend of Scottish scenery. The mountain on the left is Schiehallion, 1083m/3553ft.

78 Having travelled west from Blair Atholl up Strath Tummel, we reach the village of Kinloch Rannoch in remote north-western Perthshire. In former times it used to be less so, as it was on a route to the

west along the shores of Loch Rannoch, above. The distant mountains are 30 miles away in Glen Coe, Lochaber – but that's another story and another tour…

Published 2009 by Ness Publishing, 47 Academy Street, Elgin, Moray, IV30 1LR
Phone/fax 01343 549663 www.nesspublishing.co.uk

All photographs © Colin and Eithne Nutt except pp.7 & 23 © Scotavia Images; pp.26 & 27 © Scone Palace;
p.33 © Mike Caldwell; pp.40/41 © Kathy Collins; p.62 (both) © Scottish Wildlife Trust; p.75 © Blair Castle
Text © Colin Nutt

ISBN 978-1-906549-06-0

Front cover: Perth from Queen's Bridge; p.1: cottage in Fortingall; p.4: statuesque lady in Perth;
this page: metal-sculpted porter at Pitlochry station; back cover: 1809 bridge, Dunkeld

**For a list of websites and phone numbers please turn over >**